Every day's a Handwriting day with CGP!

Learning how to write neatly is a really important part of primary school — and in Year 2, it's all about joining those letters together...

Luckily, this CGP book is packed with fun and colourful handwriting exercises to help pupils build their skills. There's one for every day of autumn term.

And of course, we've included guidelines and plenty of examples to keep pupils' letters and words in shape. They'll be expert joiners in no time!

Contents

Use the tick boxes to help keep a record of which pages have been attempted.

Published by CGP

ISBN: 978 1 78908 545 7

Editors: Eleanor Crabtree, Mary Falkner, Rob Hayman, Sharon Keeley-Holden, Camilla Sheridan and Hayley Thompson.
Reviewers: Stephanie Lake and Adele Lemin.

With thanks to Gareth Mitchell and Glenn Rogers for the proofreading.

Cover image and graphics used throughout the book © www.edu-clips.com.

Printed by Elanders Ltd, Newcastle upon Tyne.
Based on the classic CGP style created by Richard Parsons.

How to Use this Book

- This book contains 60 pages of daily handwriting practice.
- It's split into 12 sections — that's roughly one section for each week of the Year 2 Autumn term.
- A week is made up of 5 pages, so there's one for every school day of the term (Monday – Friday).
- Each page should take about 10 minutes to complete.
- The term starts off by recapping the alphabet, capital letters and numbers. The rest of the term introduces joined-up writing. Pupils practise the joins between letters by tracing and copying letter pairs and whole words.
- A typical page looks like this:

The Week and the Day are shown at the top of the page.

Simple instructions are given in the box at the top of the page. Some pupils may need help with reading these.

Pupils first trace over the light blue letters before forming the letters themselves.

Helpful examples are often included. Arrows give guidance on correct letter and join formation.

Red dots show where to start each letter pair or word.

Pupils can assess how well they've done by colouring in a face.

If you are a parent or guardian using this book at home with your child, you should bear in mind that different schools have different handwriting styles. You should check with the school to see how they write and join each letter. Some schools also have different break letters (letters that don't join to other letters). For example, 'g' can be a break letter or can be joined. You should check which break letters the school uses.

Week 1 — Day 1

Before you get on to joined-up writing, trace each letter and then copy it. A red dot shows where to start each letter.

1. a b c
2. d e f
3. g h i j
4. k l m n
5. o p q r
6. s t u v
7. w x y z

How well did you do?

Week 1 — Day 2

The words below are really useful.
Practise tracing and copying them.
Each word should start at a red dot.

1. you you

2. your your

3. she she

4. they they

5. here here

6. there there

7. where where

How neatly did you write these words?

Week 1 — Day 3

Trace and copy these words.
Start each word at a red dot.
Check each letter touches the correct lines.

1. ask ask
2. love love

3. come come
4. some some
5. one one

6. once once
7. friend friend

How well did you do?

Week 1 — Day 4

Trace and copy these words. Start each one at a red dot. All the tall letters apart from 't' should reach the top line.

put

1. put put
2. push push
3. pull pull
4. full full
5. our our
6. house house
7. school school

How did you get on with these words?

Week 1 — Day 5

Trace and copy this sentence. It has all the letters of the alphabet in it. Red dots show you where to start the words.

Five magical wizards in

Five magica wizards in

purple cloaks turned

the bossy queen into a

yellow fox for a joke.

Did you write this sentence neatly?

Week 2 — Day 1

Trace and copy these capital letters. You'll need to take your pencil off the page for most of these letters.

1. A A B B C C

2. D D E E F F

3. G G H H I I

4. J J K K

5. L L M M

6. N N O O P P

7. Q Q R R

How did you get on with today's capital letters?

Week 2 — Day 2

Trace and copy these capital letters. Then, trace and copy the places and names at the bottom of the page.

1. S S T T U U

2. V V W W

3. X X Y Y Z Z

4. France France

5. Grace Grace

6. Wigan Wigan

7. Hamza Hamza

How did you do with these letters and words?

Week 2 — Day 3

Trace over these numbers, then copy them out.
Start each number at the red dot.

1  1 1 2 2 3 3

2 4 4 5 5 6 6

3 7 7 8 8 9 9

4 10 10 11 11

5 12 12 13 13

6 14 14 15 15

7 16 16 17 17

Could you trace and copy all of these numbers?

Week 2 — Day 4

Here are some more numbers for you to trace and copy. Every number should touch the top line.

18

1. 18 18 . . 19 19 . .

2. 20 20 . . . .
3. 1 . 2 . 3 . 4 .
4. 5 . 6 . 7 . 8 .
5. 9 . 10 . 11 . 12 .
6. 13 . 14 . 15 . 16 .
7. 17 . 18 . 19 . 20 .

How do you think you did today?

Week 2 — Day 5

Trace over these sentences about autumn.
After that, copy them out on the lines below.

Autumn starts in September.

Leaves start to change colour.

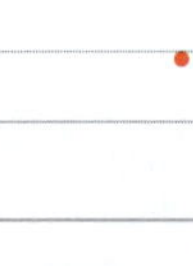

Bonfire Night is in November.

How did today's page go?

Week 3 — Day 1

These pairs of letters are connected by the first join.
Trace and copy each pair. Start at a red dot each time.

1. an an an

2. iv iv iv
3. ny ny ny
4. mm mm mm
5. ci ci ci

6. hu hu hu
7. lp lp lp

How did you get on with the first join?

Week 3 — Day 2

Trace and copy these letter pairs.
They are connected by the first join.
Start at a red dot each time.

1. tu tu
2. ar ar
3. di di
4. ip ip
5. mp mp

6. cr cr
7. nn nn

How well did you do with this join today?

Week 3 — Day 3

These words contain the first join.
Trace and then copy them.
Start at a red dot each time.

mum

1 mum mum

2 nip nip

3 any any

4 cup cup

5 tin tin

6 hip hip

7 hump hump

How did you get on with these words?

Week 3 — Day 4

Trace and copy these words,
which contain the first join.
Each word should start at a red dot.

din

1. din din

2. air air

3. kip kip

4. hum hum

5. imp imp

6. tiny tiny

7. dummy dummy

How neatly did you join your letters?

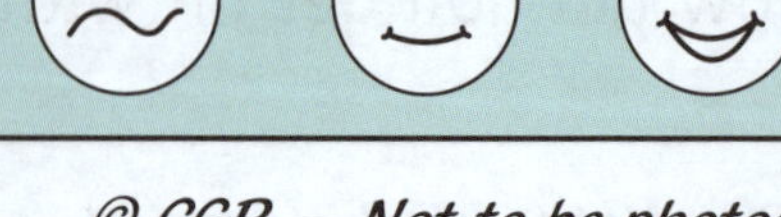

Week 3 — Day 5

Trace and copy these letter pairs.
They are connected by the second join.
Each pair should start at a red dot.

1. ct ct ct
2. al al al

3. mb mb mb
4. uf uf uf
5. ch ch ch
6. nk nk nk
7. it it it

How did you get on with this join?

Week 4 — Day 1

Each of these letter pairs is connected by the second join. Trace them and then copy them out. Start at a red dot each time.

1. ab ab

2. ck ck

3. il il

4. ut ut

5. if if

6. th th

7. lk lk

How happy are you with this join?

Week 4 — Day 2

All of the words below have the second join in them. Trace each word and then copy it out. Start at a red dot.

all

1 all all

2 cut cut

3 mill mill

4 ink ink

5 chin chin

6 club club

7 climb climb

Did you trace and copy these words neatly?

Week 4 — Day 3

Trace each of the words below, then copy them out. Don't forget to cross the 't's and dot the 'i's too.

ant

1. ant ant
2. kit kit
3. ill ill

4. nut nut
5. milk milk

6. aunt aunt
7. think think

How did you get on with these words?

Week 4 — Day 4

These letters are connected by the third join.
Trace each pair, then copy it out. You'll need
to go back on yourself to do the second letter.

1. ic ic ic

2. ka ka ka

3. co co co

4. ha ha ha

5. ld ld ld

6. ac ac ac

7. dg dg dg

How did you get on with this join?

Week 4 — Day 5

Each of these pairs of letters is connected by the third join. Trace them, then copy them out.

1. mo mo

2. eq eq

3. tc tc

4. id id

5. ng ng

6. ud ud

7. aq aq

How did you find this page?

Week 5 — Day 1

These words all contain the third join.
Carefully trace and copy each one.

car

1. car car

2. do do

3. hand hand

4. click click

5. lady lady

6. child child

7. duck duck

How did you get on with this join?

Week 5 — Day 2

The words on this page contain the third join. Trace and copy them all.

luck

1. luck luck

2. into into

3. chair chair

4. mind mind

5. hair hair

6. king king

7. talking talking

Could you trace and copy all of these words?

Week 5 — Day 3

Today's page is about practising the third join to an 's'. The join is made in the same way but it is longer. The 's' tilts a bit too.

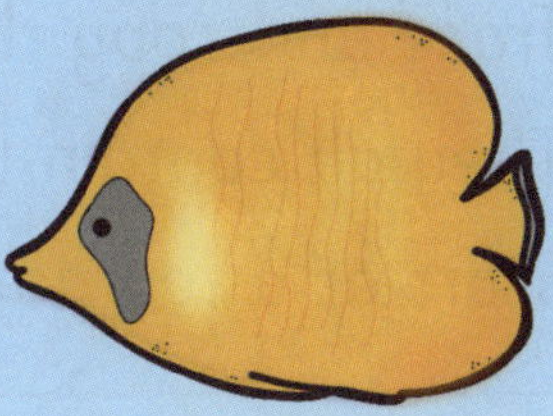

1. as as

2. is is

3. ls ls

4. ds ds

5. ns ns

6. ms ms

7. ks ks

How did you do with writing these letters?

Week 5 — Day 4

Trace and copy the words below.
They all contain the third join to an 's'.
Start at a red dot each time.

kits

1. kits kits

2. cats cats

3. calls calls

4. thanks thanks

5. tails tails

6. lands lands

7. llamas llamas

How did you find copying today's words?

Week 5 — Day 5

Here are some letter pairs that all contain the fourth join. Trace over each pair first, then copy it out.

1. ru ru ru
2. or or or
3. rp rp rp
4. ov ov ov

5. ri ri ri
6. op op op

7. vi vi vi

Could you trace and copy this join neatly?

Week 6 — Day 1

These letter pairs are all connected by the fourth join. Trace them and then copy them. Make sure to start each pair at a red dot.

1  rn rn

2 ow ow

3 rm rm

4  wn wn

5 oi oi

6 wi wi

7 ry ry

How did you find writing today's join?

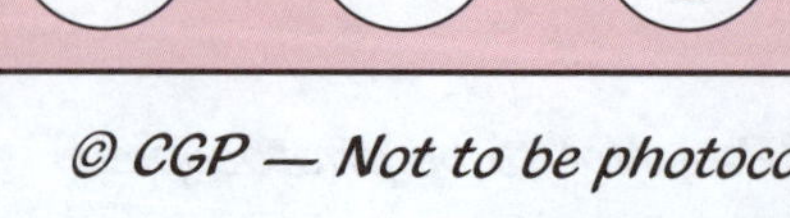

Week 6 — Day 2

Trace and copy these words that all contain the fourth join.

corn

1. corn corn

2. arm arm

3. witch witch

4. hour hour

5. town town

6. wing wing

7. ruin ruin

How did you do today?

Week 6 — Day 3

Here are some words to help you practise the fourth join. Trace over them once and then copy them out.

coin

1. coin coin

2. harp harp

3. top top

4. drum drum

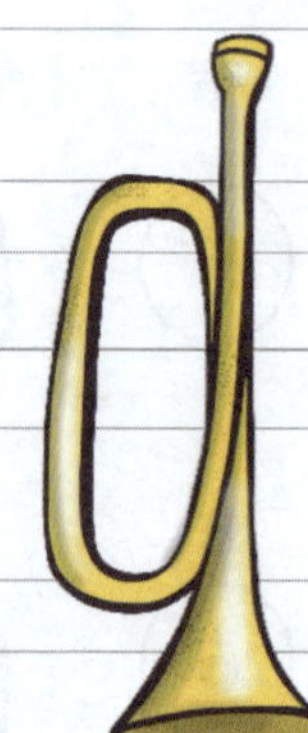

5. horn horn

6. know know

7. diary diary

How did you get on with this join?

Week 6 — Day 4

Trace and copy the pairs of letters below. To do the fourth join from an 'f', you need to lift your pencil off the page.

1. fi fi fi
2. fr fr fr

3. fu fu fu
4. fy fy fy

5. fi fu
6. fr fy
7. fi fu fr fy

How did you get on with this join?

Week 6 — Day 5

Use these words to practise your fourth joins from 'f'. Start each word at a red dot.

full

1. full full

2. find find

3. fun fun

4. fur fur

5. fruit fruit

6. comfy comfy

7. fiction fiction

Could you neatly write these words?

Week 7 — Day 1

These pairs of letters are joined by the fifth join.
Trace over them, then copy them out.

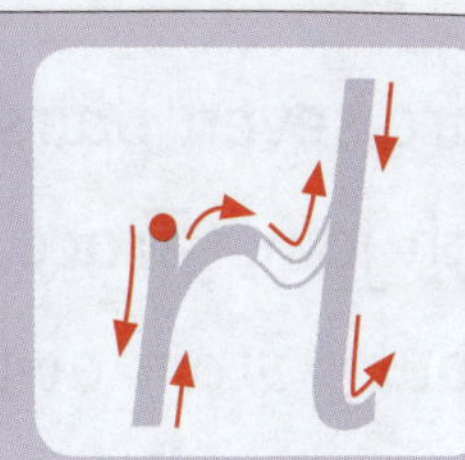

1. rl rl rl

2. ot ot ot

3. ob ob ob

4. wl wl wl

5. rt rt rt

6. oh oh oh

7. wh wh wh

Could you trace today's join neatly?

Week 7 — Day 2

Here are seven pairs of letters joined by the fifth join. Trace them, then copy them out. Start at the red dot each time.

1. rb rb
2. ok ok

3. wt wt

4. of of
5. ol ol
6. rf rf

7. rk rk

How did you do with today's join?

Week 7 — Day 3

Trace and copy these words.
They all contain the fifth join.

cold

1. cold cold

2. howl howl

3. who who

4. art art

5. dot dot

6. dark dark

7. holiday holiday

Could you write these words neatly?

Week 7 — Day 4

Practise the fifth join by tracing and then copying the words on this page.

what

1. what what
2. curly curly

3. lot lot

4. dirty dirty
5. court court
6. knot knot

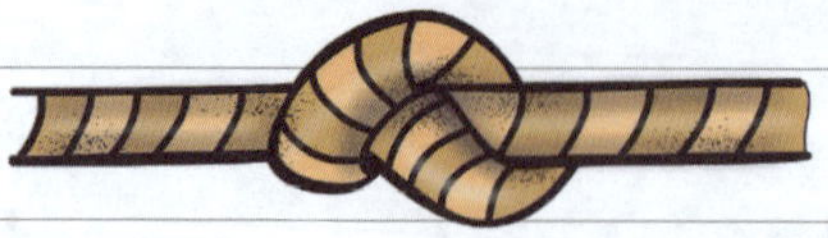

7. colour colour

How did you do with these words?

Week 7 — Day 5

These pairs of letters and words all have a fifth join that goes from 'f' to another tall letter. Trace them all and then copy them.

1 fl fl fl

2 ft ft ft

3 fh fh fh

4 ff ff ff

5 fb fb fb

6 off flag

7 flop tuft

How well did you do today?

Week 8 — Day 1

Trace these words and then copy them out. In each word, the letter 'f' joins to a tall letter using the fifth join.

1. fly fly
2. lift lift

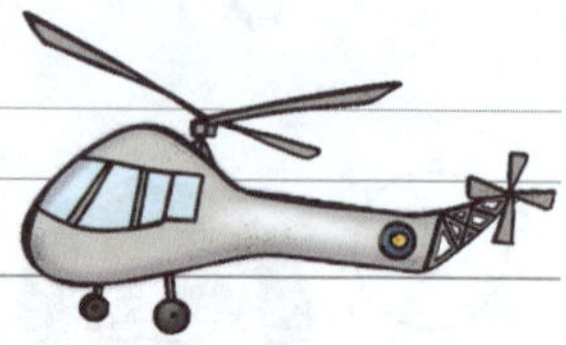

3. flat flat
4. cliff cliff

5. flip flip
6. fluffy fluffy
7. drift drift

How did you get on with this page?

Week 8 — Day 2

Try tracing and copying these letter pairs with the sixth join. Start at the red dot each time.

1. ro ro ro

2. wa wa wa

3. og og og

4. oo oo oo

5. rd rd rd

6. oa oa oa

7. rc rc rc

How did you find the sixth join?

Week 8 — Day 3

Practise the sixth join by tracing and copying each pair of letters.

1. va va

2. oq oq

3. ra ra

4. wd wd

5. oc oc

6. rg rg

7. vo vo

How did you get on with joining these letters?

Week 8 — Day 4

All of these words have the sixth join in them. Trace them first and then copy them.

door

1. door door
2. arch arch
3. word word
4. lava lava
5. clog clog

6. floor floor
7. frog frog

How did you find these words?

Week 8 — Day 5

In the words below, 'f' joins to the next letter using the sixth join. Trace each word and then copy it out.

food

1. food food
2. fact fact
3.  farm farm
4. fold fold
5. fairy fairy 
6. four four
7. 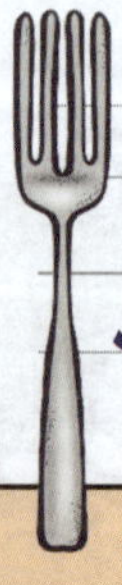 fork fork

How did this page go?

Week 9 — Day 1

These words will help you practise your sixth join to 's'.
Trace each word once, then copy it.

ours

1. ours ours

2. cars cars

3. throws throws

4. doors doors

5. arrows arrows

6. roars roars

7. chairs

Were you able to neatly trace and copy this join?

Week 9 — Day 2

Trace and copy the seven words below to practise all the different sixth joins.

rain

1 rain rain

2 foot foot

3 family family

4 lord lord

5 watch watch

6 draws draws

7 cocoa cocoa

How did you do today?

Week 9 — Day 3

When you join from the bottom of a letter to an 'e', the 'e' tilts slightly. Trace and copy these pairs of letters to practise this join.

1. ne ne ne
2. ce ce ce
3. me me me
4. le le le

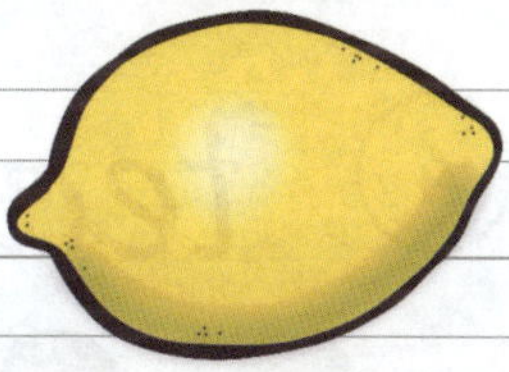

5. te te te
6. ie ie ie
7. de de de

Pick a face to show how you did today.

Week 9 — Day 4

Trace and copy the words below.
Focus on getting the join to the letter 'e' right.

one

1. one one

2. mice mice

3. ride ride

4. tea tea

5. time time

6. hole hole

7. alien alien

Did you trace and copy these words neatly?

Week 9 — Day 5

This page has joins to 'e' from the top of the last letter.
It also has joins to 'e' from the letter 'f'.
The 'e' doesn't tilt here. Trace and copy each letter pair.

1. ve ve ve

2. oe oe oe

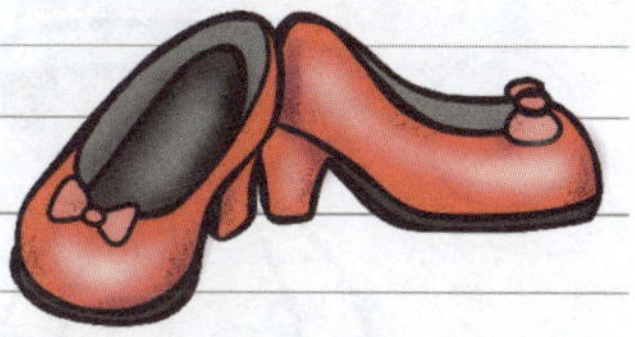

3. fe fe fe

4. we we we

5. re re re

6. ve ve oe oe

7. fe we re

How do you think you did with today's joins?

Week 10 — Day 1

Practise joining to the letter 'e' by tracing and copying these words.

real

1. real real

2. well well

3. toe toe

4. very very

5. wife wife

6. few few

7. hive hive

How did the joins on this page go?

Week 10 — Day 2

Here are some more words for you to practise joining to the letter 'e'.

here

1. here here

2. reed reed

3. every every

4. feet feet

5. were were

6. free free

7. leave leave

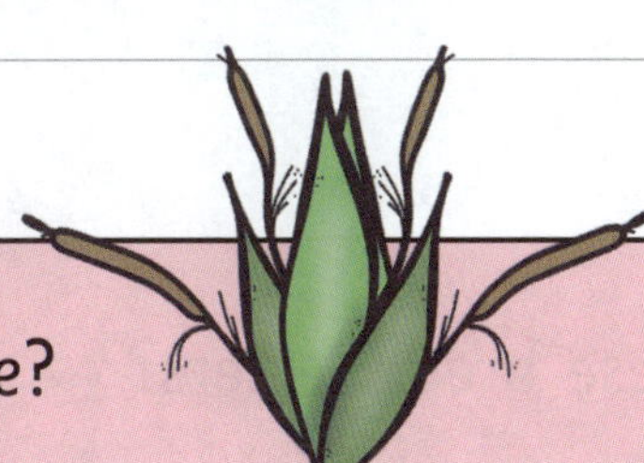

How did you find this page?

Week 10 — Day 3

Break letters don't join to the next letter. These words all start with the break letter 'b', 'j' or 'g'. Trace and copy them.

both

1. both both

2. judo judo
3. great great

4. bacon bacon
5. jive jive
6. bunk bunk
7. gold gold

How did you get on with these break letters?

Week 10 — Day 4

Trace and copy these words. Each one starts with the break letter 's', 'p' or 'q'.

sure

1. sure sure
2. play play

3. quack quack
4. steak steak
5. quiet quiet
6. plant plant
7. school school

How easy did you find this page?

Week 10 — Day 5

The final three break letters are 'x', 'y' and 'z'. Try tracing and copying some words starting with these letters.

1. yes yes
2. zoom zoom
3. zero zero
4. your your
5. zip zip
6. year year
7. xylophone

How did these words go?

Week 11 — Day 1

Trace and copy the words below. These words all include break letters in the middle.

rabbit

1. rabbit rabbit 
2. apple apple 
3.  enjoy enjoy
4. trumpet trumpet
5. forest forest 
6. right right
7. squid squid 

Could you trace and copy these words neatly? 

Week 11 — Day 2

Trace and copy these seven words with break letters. Make sure you start each word at a red dot.

extra

1. extra extra

2. wizard wizard

3. freeze freeze

4. myth myth

5. excited excited

6. flying flying

7. lizard lizard

How did you do with today's words?

Week 11 — Day 3

Trace and copy these words.
They all have lots of break letters.

pizza

1. pizza pizza

2. squeeze squeeze
3. boxes boxes

4. zebras zebras
5. penguin penguin

6. yogurt yogurt
7. zombie zombie

How do you think you did today?

Week 11 — Day 4

Trace and copy these names and places. You will need to take your pencil off the paper to write the capital letters.

Wales

1 Wales Wales

2 Arlo Arlo

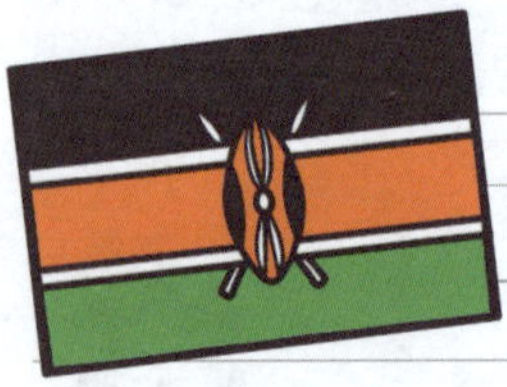

3 Kenya Kenya

4 Imogen Imogen

5 Belfast Belfast

6 Eilidh Eilidh

7 Mexico Mexico

Did you neatly write these names and places?

Week 11 — Day 5

Here are seven words to do with Christmas.
Trace them and then copy them out.

1 reindeer reindeer

2 elf elf

3 nativity nativity

4  tinsel tinsel

5 turkey turkey

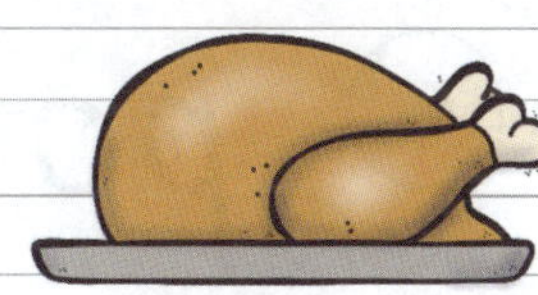

6  stocking

7 Christmas

Did you neatly trace and copy all these words?

Week 12 — Day 1

Trace and copy these words.
They all begin with 'p'.

prove

1. prove prove

2. people people

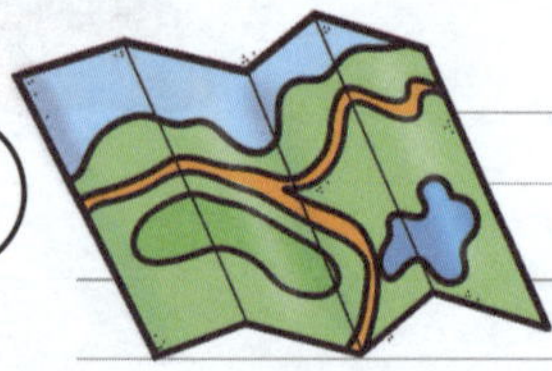

3. path path

4. parents parents

5. poor poor

6. pretty pretty

7. plant plant

How did you find these words?

Week 12 — Day 2

Try tracing and copying these words.
Watch out for the break letters.

eye

1. eye eye

2. any any

3. many many

4. busy busy

5. every every

6. body body

7. money money

How did you get on with these words?

Week 12 — Day 3

Practise joining an 'f' by tracing and copying these words.

floor

1. floor floor
2. father father
3. half half

4. after after
5. fast fast
6. find find

7. beautiful

How did you find the joins to 'f'?

Week 12 — Day 4

Try to trace and copy each word neatly. If 's' is joined to the letter before, it is tilted a bit. An 's' is also a break letter.

mess

1. mess mess
2. class class
3. grass grass

4. pass pass
5. most most
6. past past

7. last last

How did the words on this page go?

Week 12 — Day 5

Trace and copy this story.
Make sure you join the letters together neatly. Watch out for break letters.

elf

Sam was a naughty elf.

He didn't help the other elves.

He played with the ribbons

and climbed on the gifts.

How did you find this page about Sam?

E2HWAU11